Calendar No. 28

114TH CONGRESS		REPORT
1st Session	SENATE	114–32

CYBERSECURITY INFORMATION SHARING ACT OF 2015

APRIL 15, 2015.—Ordered to be printed

Mr. BURR, from the Select Committee on Intelligence,
submitted the following

R E P O R T

together with

ADDITIONAL VIEWS

[To accompany S. 754]

The Select Committee on Intelligence, having considered an original bill (S. 754) to improve cybersecurity in the United States through enhanced sharing of information about cybersecurity threats, and for other purposes, reports favorably thereon and recommends that the bill do pass.

BACKGROUND AND NEED FOR LEGISLATION

Over the last several years, the Committee has listened with increasing alarm to the testimony of senior intelligence officials and private sector experts about the growing cybersecurity threats to our nation.

The Committee has already seen the impact these threats are having on the nation's security and its economy as losses to consumers, businesses, and the government from cyber attacks, penetrations, and disruptions already total billions of dollars. Beyond direct monetary losses, the continuing efforts of foreign actors to steal intellectual property will have far reaching impacts on the innovation upon which a robust economy and strong military relies. The Committee has seen widespread theft through cyberspace increasingly evolve into disruptive and destructive attacks. American financial institutions have been subjected to denial of service attacks by foreign actors that blocked consumers' access to banking services. Critical infrastructure companies abroad and businesses in the United States have seen their vital business systems rendered useless by hostile actors operating in other countries. The reported destructive cyberattacks on the Las Vegas Sands Corporation and Sony Pictures Entertainment represent further escalation of this disturbing trend, including unprecedented efforts to destroy data of U.S. companies. Our nation is growing more vulnerable to cyber threats. Every aspect of society is growing more dependent on computers which are all linked to networks, opening this country up to many known vulnerabilities and many yet to be discovered.

The Committee and its staff have also engaged in hundreds of conversations with senior government and private sector officials that have demonstrated the need for a legislative effort to allow for the increased sharing of information about these cyber threats. There are many stakeholders who are engaged on these issues and the Committee is convinced that legislation is needed to assist them in finding better ways to work together to address our nation's shared cybersecurity challenges. This legislation is designed to create a *voluntary* cybersecurity information sharing process that will encourage public and private sector entities to share cyber threat information, removing legal barriers and the threat of unnecessary litigation. This in turn allows for greater cooperation and collaboration in the face of growing cybersecurity threats to national and economic security. Additionally, the Committee believes that such increased sharing will drive public and private sector cybersecurity efforts to develop key new technologies and processes, such as an improved ability to share technical threat information through an automated process in ''real time'' to counter cyber threats at machine speed.

Through the Committee's oversight of the Intelligence Community, it has long recognized the need to better use the government's knowledge and expertise about cyber threats for defensive purposes. This legislation includes requirements for the government to share more information, including classified information under appropriate safeguards, with relevant private sector entities to further cybersecurity. Often as a result of overclassification and parochialism, some cybersecurity information that could enable the businesses facing these threats to better protect themselves remains exclusively in the government. Although sensitive sources and methods must be protected, the government does not presently share adequate information about cyber threats. This bill encourages the government to expand this sharing and to create the appropriate processes to do so.

This legislation also includes positive legal authorities for private companies to: (1) monitor their networks, or those of their customers upon authorization and written consent, for cybersecurity purposes; (2) take defensive measures to stop cyber attacks and (3) share cyber threat information with each other and with the government to further collective cybersecurity. Through extensive hearings, briefings, and discussions, the Committee has identified the need to provide carefully tailored cybersecurity authorities to address these current gaps. The Committee also recognizes the careful balance that must be struck in providing increased authorities to ensure they are used appropriately. This legislation creates a completely voluntary information-sharing framework that includes several layers of privacy protections to prevent abuse and ensure that the government cannot inappropriately acquire or use sensitive information other than for limited cybersecurity and public safety purposes.

In addition to concerns about legal authorities, the specter of litigation for monitoring a company's own networks or sharing cyber threat indicators or defensive measures for cybersecurity purposes has disincentivized private sector cybersecurity efforts. Entities appropriately monitoring their systems for cybersecurity threats and sharing information necessary to protect against those threats should not be exposed to costly legal uncertainty for doing so. Moreover, it is these same companies who are the victims of malicious cyber activity, and their appropriate efforts to protect themselves and other future victims from cyber threats should not only be authorized but protected from unnecessary litigation. This legislation creates narrowly tailored liability protection to incentivize companies' efforts to identify cybersecurity threats and share information about them. However, this liability protection does not extend to defensive measures, nor does it protect unauthorized monitoring or sharing, including gross negligence or willful misconduct, that risks sensitive data rather than safeguarding it.

The Committee believes that the increased information sharing enabled by this bill is critical step forward for improving cybersecurity in America.

SECTION-BY-SECTION ANALYSIS AND EXPLANATION

The following is a section-by-section analysis and explanation of the Cybersecurity Information Sharing Act of 2015 that is being reported by the Committee.

Section 1. Short title

Section 1 states that this Act may be cited as the "Cybersecurity Information Sharing Act of 2015."

Section 2. Definitions

Section 2 provides 18 definitions for this Act, to include the following key terms: "cybersecurity purpose," "cybersecurity threat," "cyber threat indicator," "defensive measure," and "monitor."

The term "cybersecurity purpose" means the purpose of protecting an information system or information that is stored on, processed by, or transiting an information system from a cybersecurity threat or security vulnerability. This definition ensures that the authorities of private entities to monitor and operate defensive measures must be exercised for the purpose of protecting their own networks and those of their customers when authorized by the written consent of such customers. The definition of "cybersecurity purpose" is also one of the main limitations on the ability of private and governmental entities to use cyber threat indicators and defensive measures.

The term "cybersecurity threat" is defined as an action, not protected by the First Amendment to the Constitution of the United States, on or through an information system that may result in an unauthorized effort to adversely impact the security, availability, confidentiality, or integrity of an information system that is stored on, processed by, or transiting an information system. The term does not include any action that solely involves a violation of a consumer term of service or a consumer licensing agreement. Many terms of service agreements prohibit activities that would also meet the ''cybersecurity threat'' definition; such activities would still be considered a ''cybersecurity threat'' because they were not ''solely'' violations of consumer agreements. The Committee intends this definition to include activities that may have unauthorized and negative results, but to exclude authorized activities, such as extensive use of bandwidth that may incidentally cause adverse effects. However, this definition clearly does not permit hackers to cloak their criminal actions like theft of information or destruction of property under the ambit of First Amendment protected activities.

The term ''cyber threat indicator'' is one of the most important definitions in this Act. It is defined as information that is necessary to describe or identify: (1) malicious reconnaissance, including anomalous patterns of communications that appear to be transmitted for the purpose of gathering technical information related to a cybersecurity threat or security vulnerability; (2) a method of defeating a security control or exploitation of a security vulnerability; (3) a security vulnerability, including anomalous activity that appears to indicate the existence of a security vulnerability; (4) a method of causing a user with legitimate access to an information system or information that is stored on, processed by, or transiting an information system to unwittingly enable the defeat of a security control or exploitation of a security vulnerability; (5) malicious cyber command and control; (6) the actual or potential harm caused by an incident, including a description of the information exfiltrated as a result of a particular cybersecurity threat; (7) any other attribute of a cybersecurity threat, if disclosure of such attribute is not otherwise prohibited by law; or (8) any combination thereof. This narrow definition is a key privacy protection in the Act because it creates an exhaustive list of the types of cyber threat information that can be shared among private and governmental entities, and only when they are necessary to describe or identify threats to information and information systems. Essentially, this definition limits the information that can be shared under this Act to the techniques and ''malware'' used by malicious actors to compromise the computer networks of their victims, not sensitive personal and business information contained in such networks.

The term ''defensive measure'' is defined as an action, device, procedure, signature, technique, or other measure applied to an information system or information that is stored on, processed by, or transiting an information system that detects, prevents, or mitigates a known or suspected cybersecurity threat or security vulnerability. However, a defensive measure does not include a measure that destroys, renders unusable, or substantially harms an information system or data on an information system not belonging to the private entity operating such measure or another entity or Federal entity that is authorized to provide consent and has provided consent to that private entity for operation of such measure. Recognizing the inherent right of self-defense that entities have to protect their networks and data, the Committee intends for this definition to provide a positive legal authority allowing private entities to take measures to take appropriate steps to defend their own information networks and systems, or those of their customers when authorized by the written consent of such customers, against malicious cybersecurity threats. For example, a defensive measure could be something as simple as a security device that protects or limits access to a private entity's computer infrastructure or as complex as using sophisticated software tools to detect and protect against anomalous and unauthorized activities on a private entity's information system. Regardless, this definition does not authorize the use of measures that are generally to be considered ''offensive'' in nature, such as unauthorized access of or executing computer code on another entity's information systems or taking an action that would substantially harm another private entity's information systems. The Committee is aware that defensive measures on one entity's network could have effects on other networks. It is the Committee's intent that the authorization in this Act extends to defensive measures on an entity's information systems that do not cause substantial harm to another entity's information systems or data on such systems, regardless of whether such non-substantial harm was intended or foreseen by the implementing entity.

The term ''monitor'' means to acquire, identify, or scan, or to possess, information that is stored on, processed by, or transiting an information system. This definition, as used in this Act, is not intended to equate to the meaning of the term ''monitor'' used in the context of the interception of communications under the Federal criminal wiretap statutes or electronic surveillance under the Foreign Intelligence Surveillance Act. Specifically, private entities are only authorized to monitor *their own information systems* or those of another private entity upon the authorization and written consent of such other entity. Moreover, such monitoring is limited to cybersecurity purposes. Essentially, these important limitations ensure that private entities are only authorized to monitor their information systems to protect against cybersecurity threats and vulnerabilities. Any other monitoring would require lawful authority other than that provided in this Act.

Section 3. Sharing of Information by the Federal Government

Section 3 requires the Director of National Intelligence, the Secretary of Homeland Security, the Secretary of Defense, and the Attorney General to develop and promulgate procedures that facilitate and promote the timely sharing of: (1) classified cyber threat indicators with cleared representatives of relevant entities; (2) declassified cyber threat indicators with relevant entities; (3) unclassified cyber threat indicators with relevant entities or the public; and (4) information in the possession of the Federal Government about cybersecurity threats to such entities to prevent or mitigate adverse effects from such cybersecurity threats. These procedures must ensure that the Federal government has and maintains the capability to share cyber threat indicators in real time consistent with the protection of classified information and incorporate to the greatest extent practicable existing processes and existing roles and responsibilities.

The procedures required by this section must also include a process for notifying entities that have received a cyber threat indicator from a Federal entity that is known or determined to be in error or in contravention of Federal law or policy. Federal entities receiving cyber threat indicators will also be required to implement and use security controls to protect against unauthorized access to or acquisition of such indicators. Moreover, the procedures require that a Federal entity, prior to sharing a cyber threat indicator, review and remove any information that the Federal entity knows at the time of the sharing to be personal information of or identifying a specific person not directly related to a cybersecurity threat or implement and use a technical capability configured to remove personal information of or identifying a specific person not directly related to a cybersecurity threat. In developing these procedures, the responsible officials must coordinate with other appropriate Federal entities, including the National Laboratories due to their technical expertise, so that effective protocols are implemented to facilitate and promote sharing in a timely manner. Within 60 days of the enactment of this Act, the Director of National Intelligence in consultation with the heads of the appropriate Federal entities shall submit these procedures to the Congress.

Section 4. Authorizations for Preventing, Detecting, Analyzing, and Mitigating Cybersecurity Threats

Subsection (a) of Section 4 provides a private entity with the authority to monitor, for cybersecurity purposes: (1) its own information systems; (2) an information system of another entity, upon the authorization and written consent of such other entity; (3) an information system of a Federal entity, upon the authorization and written consent of an authorized representative of the Federal entity; and (4) information that is stored on, processed by, or transiting an information system monitored by the private entity. Nothing in subsection (a) shall be construed to authorize the monitoring of information systems, or the use of any information obtained through such monitoring of such information systems, other than as provided in this Act.

Subsection (b) provides private entities with the authority to operate defensive measures, for cybersecurity purposes, that are applied to its information systems to protect the rights and property of such private entities, those of another entity upon written consent of such entity for operation of such defensive measures to protect the rights and property of that entity, or those of a Federal entity upon written consent of an authorized representative of such Federal entity for operation of such defensive measures to protect the rights or property of the Federal Government. This subsection does not authorize the use of defensive measures other than for cybersecurity purposes.

Under subsection (c), an entity is authorized to share with or receive from any other entity or the Federal Government cyber threat indicators and defensive measures for the purposes permitted under this Act, consistent with the protection of classified information when applicable. An entity receiving cyber threat indicators and defensive measures from another entity or Federal entity must comply with otherwise lawful restrictions placed on the sharing or use of such cyber threat indicators or defensive measures by the sharing entity or Federal entity, such as a limitation of future sharing of the indicators or measures.

An entity monitoring information systems, operating defensive measures or providing or receiving defensive measures under Section 4 must implement and utilize security controls to protect against unauthorized access to or acquisition of such cyber threat indicators or defensive measures.

Prior to sharing a cyber threat indicator pursuant to this Act, an entity shall review such cyber threat indicator to assess whether such indicator contains any information that the entity knows at the time of sharing to be personal information of or identifying a specific person not directly related to a cybersecurity threat and remove such information or implement and utilize a technical capability configured to remove any information contained with such indicator that the entity knows at the time of the sharing to be personal information of or identifying a specific person not directly related to a cybersecurity threat. During the Committee's drafting of the legislation, industry groups and trade associations noted that the requirement to remove personal information may preclude some companies, especially smaller ones, from participating in the information sharing process endorsed by the bill. As a private entity must ensure that any information shared meets the definition for ''cyber threat indicator'' or ''defensive measure'' to comply with the Act, the requirement to remove any known unnecessary privacy information strikes the appropriate balance between narrowly tailoring what information can be shared and providing a practicable standard. Further, the Committee hopes that the Attorney General guidance required in section 5 and common practices and guidelines will assist smaller and middle-sized companies implement this requirement.

Section 4 authorizes an entity to use cyber threat indicators and defensive measures, for cybersecurity purposes, to monitor or operate defensive measures on its information systems or those of another entity or Federal entity upon written consent.

A cyber threat indicator shared by an entity with a State, tribal, or local department or agency may, with the prior written consent of such entity, be used for the purpose of preventing, investigating, or prosecuting any of the offenses described in Section 5(d)(5)(A)(vi). These offenses involve imminent threats of death, serious bodily harm, or serious economic harm, including a terrorist act or a use of a weapon of mass destruction. They also include serious violent felonies and offenses related to fraud and identity theft, and protection of trade secrets. If the need for immediate use prevents a State, tribal, or local department or agency from obtaining written consent before such use, consent may be provided orally with subsequent documentation of consent. The entity providing consent for this use must have the authorization to possess and share such a cyber threat indicator under this Act and must conduct such sharing consistent with the conditions set out.

Cyber threat indicators shared with a State, tribal, or local department or agency under Section 4 are deemed voluntarily shared information and exempt from disclosure under any State, tribal, or local law requiring disclosure of information or records.

In general, cyber threat indicators shared with a State, tribal, or local government under this Act shall not be directly used by any State, tribal, or local government to regulate, which includes bringing an enforcement action, the lawful activity of any entity, including an activity relating to monitoring, operating a defensive measure, or sharing of a cyber threat indicator. However, a cyber threat indicator or defensive measure may, consistent with a State, tribal, or local government regulatory authority specifically relating to the prevention or mitigation of cybersecurity threats to information systems, inform the development or implementation of a regulation relating to such information systems. The Committee views this as a narrow exception to ensure that government agencies with regulatory authority understand the current landscape of cyber threats and those facing the particular regulatory sector over which they have cognizance.

Under subsection (e), two or more private entities are not to be considered in violation of any provision of antitrust law when exchanging or providing a cyber threat indicator, or assistance relating to the prevention, investigation, or mitigation of a cybersecurity threat, for cybersecurity purposes under this Act. This provision should be read in conjunction with the rule of construction in Section 8(e) that nothing in the Act shall be construed to permit price-fixing, allocating a market between competitors, monopolizing or attempting to monopolize a market, boycotting, or exchanges of price or cost information, customer lists, or information regarding future competitive planning. The bill allows for the sharing of cybersecurity-related information for cybersecurity purposes, acknowledging that doing so might otherwise be a potential violation of anti-trust laws that seek to limit sharing of information for other purposes. The bill does not intend to protect companies from engaging in anti-competitive behavior under the guise of cybersecurity.

Further, this subsection only applies to information that is exchanged or assistance provided to the communication or disclosure of cyber threat indicators for the facilitation of the prevention, investigation, or mitigation of cybersecurity threats to an information system or information that is stored on, processed by, or transiting an information system.

Section 4 also clarifies that the sharing of cyber threat indicators under this Act shall not create a right or benefit to similar information by such entity or another entity.

Section 5. Sharing of Cyber Threat Indicators and Defensive Measures with the Federal Government

Section 5 directs the Attorney General, in coordination with the heads of appropriate Federal entities, to develop and submit to Congress not later than 60 days after the enactment of this Act interim policies and procedures relating to the receipt of cyber threat indicators and defensive measures by the Federal Government. Not later than 180 days after the enactment of this Act, the Attorney General, in coordination with the heads of appropriate Federal entities, is required to promulgate a final version of such policies and procedures.

The policies and procedures developed under Section 5 must meet several requirements in addition to being consistent with the Attorney General's privacy and civil liberties guidelines required by subsection (b). They must ensure that cyber threat indicators shared with the Federal Government through the real time process described in subsection (c)—the capability and process within the DHS—are shared in an automated manner with all appropriate Federal entities, are not subject to any delay or interference, and may be provided to other Federal entities. The Committee intends that these policies and procedures both enable the delivery of real time information about cybersecurity threats to appropriate Federal entities and provide sufficient technical controls to protect privacy information.

For cyber threat indicators shared in a manner other than the real-time process described in subsection (c), the policies and procedures shall ensure that cyber threat indicators are shared as quickly as operationally practicable with all appropriate Federal entities, are not subject to unnecessary delay, interference, or any other action that could impede receipt by all of the appropriate Federal entities, and may be provided to other Federal entities. As cyber threat indicators received outside of the real-time process in subsection (c) may be received by the Federal Government in a format less conducive to ''as quickly as operationally practicable'' sharing, the Committee intends that this sharing requirement will vest when such information is in a format that can feasibly be shared. Once a cyber threat indicator can feasibly be shared with appropriate Federal entities, the Federal entity possessing such indicator must proceed to share it consistent with the policies and procedures and without unnecessary delay. The Attorney General's policies and procedures should include how such cyber threat indicators will be put into a shareable format and the proper sharing procedures within the Federal Government. Further, the policies and procedures shall govern the retention, use, and dissemination of cyber threat indicators shared with the Federal Government, consistent with this Act, otherwise applicable law, and consistent with the applicable sections of the commonly accepted fair information practice principles. To ensure compliance, an audit capability and appropriate sanctions for officers, employees, or agents of a Federal entity who knowingly and willfully conduct unauthorized activities are required to be included in the policies and procedures.

In an effort to assist the public and promote sharing of cyber threat indicators, Section 5 requires the Attorney General to develop and make publicly available guidance that: (1) identifies the types of information that would qualify as a cyber threat indicator under this Act that would be unlikely to include personal information of or identifying a specific person not directly related to a cyber security threat; (2) identifies the types of information that are protected under otherwise applicable privacy laws that are unlikely to be directly related to a cybersecurity threat; and (3) contains such other matters as the Attorney General considers appropriate for entities sharing cyber threat indicators with Federal entities under this Act.

Section 5 also directs the Attorney General, not later than 60 days after the date of enactment, in coordination with heads of the appropriate Federal entities and in consultation with privacy and civil liberties officers of such entities, to develop, submit to Congress, and make available to the public interim guidelines relating to privacy and civil liberties that will govern the receipt, retention, use, and dissemination of cyber threat indicators by a Federal entity obtained in connection with activities authorized under this Act. Not later than 180 days after the date of enactment, the Attorney General shall, in coordination with the heads of the appropriate Federal entities and in consultation with privacy and civil liberties officers of such entities and such private entities with industry expertise as the Attorney General considers relevant, promulgate final privacy guidelines that shall govern the receipt, retention, use, and dissemination of cyber threat indicators by a Federal entity obtained in connection with activities authorized in this Act. The Attorney General is also required to periodically review these privacy guidelines, again in coordination with the heads of the appropriate Federal entities and in consultation with privacy and civil liberties officers and industry experts. Consistent with the need to protect information from cybersecurity threats and mitigate those threats, the guidelines are required to limit the impact on privacy and civil liberties from activities by the Federal Government under this Act. These guidelines shall also limit the receipt, retention, use, and dissemination of cyber threat indicators containing personal information of or identifying specific persons. As part of these limitations, the guidelines will establish a process for the timely destruction of information that is known not to be directly related to uses authorized under this Act and specific limitations on the length of time a cyber threat indicator may be retained by the Federal Government.

The guidelines will include requirements to safeguard cyber threat indicators containing personal information of or identifying specific persons from unauthorized access or acquisition, including appropriate sanctions for activities by officers, employees, or agents of the Federal Government in contravention of such guidelines. If a Federal entity determines or knows that it has received information that does not constitute a cyber threat indicator, the guidelines shall include a procedure to notify entities and Federal entities. The privacy and civil liberties guidelines will protect the confidentiality of cyber threat indicators containing personal information of or identifying specific persons to the greatest extent practicable, and they will require recipients to be informed that such indicators may only be used for purposes authorized under this Act. They must also include steps that may be needed so that dissemination of cyber threat indicators is consistent with the protection of classified and other sensitive national security information.

Subsection (c) requires the Secretary of Homeland Security, not later than 90 days after the date of the enactment of this Act and in coordination with the heads of the appropriate Federal entities, to develop and implement a capability and process (commonly referred to as a ''portal'') within the DHS that accepts cyber threat indicators and defensive measures from any entity in real time. The Committee intends that this DHS capability should build upon current Federal Government efforts to both more efficiently receive cyber threat indicators from outside the Federal Government and to more efficiently share such indicators within the Federal Government.

Upon certification by the Secretary of Homeland Security, this capability shall be the process by which the Federal Government receives cyber threat indicators and defensive measures shared by a private entity through electronic mail or media, an interactive form on an Internet website, or a real time, automated process between information systems. There are only two exceptions to this requirement: (1) communications between a Federal entity and a private entity regarding a previously shared cyber threat indicator; and (2) communications by a regulated entity with such entity's

Federal regulatory authority regarding a cybersecurity threat. The sharing of cyber threat indicators and defensive measures in other formats where there is less privacy risk, such as a telephone call, letter, or in-person meeting, receives liability protection regardless of whether it is first sent through the DHS portal.

When cyber threat indicators and defensive measures are shared through the DHS capability, the Secretary of Homeland Security will ensure that all of the appropriate Federal entities, as defined, receive them consistent with applicable policies, procedures, and guidelines in Section 5.

The DHS capability and process does not limit or prohibit otherwise lawful disclosures of communications, records, or other information, including: (1) reporting of known or suspected criminal activity, by an entity to any other entity or a Federal entity; (2) voluntary or legally compelled participation in a Federal investigation; or (3) providing cyber threat indicators or defensive measures as part of a statutory or authorized contractual requirement.

Not later than 60 days after the date of enactment, the Secretary of Homeland Security shall submit to Congress a report on the development and implementation of the capability and process required by this section.

Subsection (d) includes a number of protections for information shared with or provided to the Federal Government. The provision of cyber threat indicators and defensive measures to the Federal Government under this Act does not constitute the waiver of any applicable privilege or protection provided by law, including trade secret protection. A cyber threat indicator or defensive measure provided by an entity to the Federal Government under this Act shall be considered the commercial, financial, and proprietary information of such entity when so designated by the originating entity. Consistent with this Act and all privileges, protections, and any claims of propriety on such cyber threat indicators or defensive measures, the Committee expects that the Federal Government will further share and use such information for cybersecurity purposes. This sharing and use will be governed by the policies, procedures, and guidelines required by Section 5. Cyber threat indicators and defensive measures provided to the Federal Government under this Act will also be deemed voluntary shared information and exempt from disclosure under section 5 U.S.C. 552 and any State, tribal, or local law requiring disclosure of information or records. Additionally, such cyber threat indicators and defensive measures shall be withheld without discretion from the public under 5 U.S.C. 552(b)(3)(B) and any State, tribal, or local law requiring disclosure of information or records. The provision of cyber threat indicators and defensive measures under this Act shall not be subject to the rules of any Federal agency or department or any judicial doctrine regarding ex parte communications with a decision-making official.

Cyber threat indicators and defensive measures provided to the Federal Government under this Act may be disclosed to, retained by, and used by, consistent with otherwise applicable Federal law, any Federal agency or department, component, officer, employee, or agent of the Federal Government solely for the purposes identified by Section 5, and consistent with the procedures developed by the Attorney General. These purposes are: (1) a cybersecurity purpose;

(2) the purpose of identifying a cybersecurity threat, including the source of such cybersecurity threat, or a security vulnerability; (3) the purpose of identifying a cybersecurity threat involving the use of an information system by a foreign adversary or terrorist; (4) the purpose of responding to, or otherwise preventing or mitigating, an imminent threat of death, serious bodily harm, or serious economic harm, including a terrorist act or a use of a weapon of mass destruction; (5) the purpose of responding to, or otherwise preventing or mitigating, a serious threat to a minor, including sexual exploitation and threats to physical safety; or (6) the purpose of preventing, investigating, disrupting, or prosecuting an offense arising out of a previously described imminent threat or any of the offenses listed in Section 5(d)(5)(vi), including offenses related to serious violent felonies, fraud and identity theft, espionage and censorship, and protection of trade secrets. The word ''imminent'' in paragraph 5(d)(5)(A)(iv) is intended to modify all the threats listed in that paragraph, to include the threat of a terrorist act or use of a weapon of mass destruction.

Use of cyber threat indicators and defensive measures by the Federal Government will be conducted in accordance with the policies, procedures, and guidelines required in Section 5, and will be done in a manner that protects from unauthorized use or disclosure any cyber threat indicators that may contain personal information of or identifying specific persons and protects the confidentiality of such information.

Additionally, such cyber threat indicators and defensive measures shared with the Federal Government under this Act shall not be directly used by any Federal, State, tribal, or local government to regulate, including an enforcement action, the lawful activities of any entity, including an activity relating to monitoring, operating a defensive measure, or sharing of a cyber threat indicator. However, a cyber threat indicator or defensive measure may, consistent with Federal or State regulatory authority specifically relating to the prevention or mitigation of cybersecurity threats to information systems, inform the development or implementation of a regulation relating to such information systems. As previously described, the Committee intends for this exception to be narrowly constrained to improving the government's understanding of cybersecurity threats. The procedures developed and implemented under this Act are not to be considered regulations within the meaning of this section.

Section 6. Protection from Liability

Subsection (a) of Section 6 provides that no cause of action shall lie or be maintained in any court against any private entity, and such action shall be promptly dismissed, for the monitoring of information systems and information under Section 4 that is conducted in accordance with this Act. The Committee intends that monitoring for cybersecurity purposes as authorized by this Act should be protected from liability to encourage private entities' efforts to identify cybersecurity threats.

Subsection (b) provides that no cause of action shall lie or be maintained in any court against any entity, and such action shall be promptly dismissed, for the sharing or receipt of cyber threat indicators or defensive measures under Section 4 when conducted in accordance with this Act, including cases in which such information is shared with the Federal Government in a manner consistent with subsection (c)(1)(B) of Section 5. Liability protection for the sharing or receipt of cyber threat indicators or defensive measures under Section 4 conducted in accordance with this Act, and in a manner consistent with subsection (c)(1)(B) of Section 5, does not go into effect until the earlier of the date on which the interim policies required under Section 5(a)(1) are submitted to Congress or the date that is 60 days after this Act's date of enactment. In all other cases where the sharing or receipt of cyber threat indicators or defensive measures is conducted in accordance with the Act, liability protection is effective immediately upon enactment of this Act. The Committee intends that the sharing between entities of cyber threat indicators and defensive measures for cybersecurity purposes in accordance with this Act, including the removal of sensitive personal information not directly related to a cybersecurity threat, should be protected from claims. Activities conducted in contravention of this Act's provisions are not entitled to such liability protection, but this Act does not create any cause of action for such non-compliance. When private entities share cyber threat indicators or defensive measures with the Federal Government in a manner consistent with subsection (c)(1)(B) of Section 5, such entities should also not be subject to burdensome litigation. The Committee intends that entities sharing such information with the Federal Government should do so consistently with required procedures to qualify for such protection.

Subsection (c) clarifies that nothing in this section shall be construed to require dismissal of a cause of action against an entity that has engaged in gross negligence or willful misconduct in the course of conducting activities authorized by this Act. Also, nothing in this section shall be construed to undermine or limit the availability of otherwise applicable common law or statutory defenses. The Committee intends to protect the responsible behavior of entities furthering cybersecurity under the authorizations and procedures of this Act, but it does not seek to protect willful or reckless activities that violate the letter and spirit of its provisions. Entities should not use Section 6 as an excuse to engage in wanton or dangerous activities, nor should they consider it to indemnify them for purposes other than the purposes authorized by this Act.

This section does not provide protections from liability arising out of a private entity's use of defensive measures, because it is the Committee's intent to maintain the status quo with respect to the use of cybersecurity defensive measures. While section 4 authorizes the use of defensive measures by an entity on its information networks or the networks of a consenting entity, the Committee notes that the use of defensive measures may have significant impact on those networks or in physical space. The lack of liability protection for the use of defensive measures should not be interpreted as the Committee taking any view on whether and how defensive measures should or should not be implemented.

Section 7. Oversight of Government Activities

Section 7 mandates reports on implementation and privacy impacts by agency heads, Inspectors General, and the Privacy Civil Liberties Oversight Board to ensure that cyber threat information is properly received, handled, and shared by the federal government.

Section 8. Construction and Preemption

Section 8 contains 19 construction provisions for this Act. Nothing in this Act shall be construed to: (1) limit or prohibit otherwise lawful disclosures of communications, records, or other information; (2) preempt any employee from exercising whistleblower rights currently provided under any law, rule, or regulation; (3) create any immunity against, or otherwise affecting, any action brought by the Federal Government to enforce any law, executive order, or procedure governing the appropriate handling, disclosure, or use of classified information; (4) affect the conduct of authorized law enforcement or intelligence activities; (5) modify the authority of the Federal Government to protect classified information and sources and methods and the national security of the United States; (6) affect any requirement under any other provision of law for an entity to provide information to the Federal Government; (7) permit price-fixing, allocating a market between competitors, monopolizing or attempting to monopolize a market, boycotting, or exchanges of price or cost information, customer lists, or information regarding future competitive planning; (8) limit or modify an existing information sharing relationship; (9) prohibit a new information sharing relationship; (10) require a new information relationship between any entity and the Federal Government; (11) require the use of the DHS capability in Section 5(c); (12) amend, repeal, or supersede any current or future contractual relationship between any entities, or between any entity and the Federal Government; (13) abrogate trade secret or intellectual property rights of any entity or Federal entity; (14) permit the Federal government to require an entity to provide information to the Federal Government; (15) permit the Federal Government to condition the sharing of cyber threat indicators with an entity on such entity's provision of cyber threat indicators to the Federal Government; (16) permit the Federal Government to condition the award of any Federal grant, contract, or purchase on the provision of a cyber threat indicator to a Federal entity; (17) subject any entity to liability for choosing not to engage in the voluntary activities authorized in this Act; (18) authorize, or to modify any existing authority of, a department or agency of the Federal Government to retain or use any information shared under this Act for any use other than permitted in this Act; or (19) limit the authority of the Secretary of Defense to develop, prepare, coordinate, or, when authorized by the President to do so, conduct a military cyber operation in response to a malicious cyber activity carried out against the United States or a United States person by a foreign government or an organization sponsored by a foreign government or a terrorist organization.

This bill supersedes any statute or other law of a State or political subdivision of a State that restricts or otherwise expressly regulates an activity authorized under this bill. However, this bill shall not be construed to supersede any statute or other law of a State or political subdivision of a State concerning the use of authorized law enforcement practices and procedures.

Nothing in this bill shall be construed to authorized the promulgation of any regulations not specifically authorized by this bill, establish any regulatory authority not specifically established under this bill, or to authorize regulatory actions that would duplicate or conflict with regulatory requirements, mandatory standards, or related processes under Federal law.

Section 9. Report on Cybersecurity Threats

Section 9 requires the Director of National Intelligence to submit a one-time report to the congressional intelligence committees on cybersecurity threats, including cyber attacks, theft, and data breaches.

Section 10. Conforming Amendments

Section 10 makes a technical amendment to 5 U.S.C. 552(b).

Section 10 also makes a conforming amendment to Section 941 of the National Defense Authorization Act for Fiscal Year 2013 (Public Law 112–239) to allow the Secretary of Defense to share information received under that section consistent with this bill.

COMMITTEE ACTION

On March 12, 2015, a quorum being present, the Committee met to consider the bill and amendments. The Committee took the following actions:

Votes on amendments to committee bill

By a voice vote, the Committee made the Chairman and Vice Chairman's bill the base text for purposes of amendment. The Committee also authorized the staff to make technical and conforming changes in the bill following the completion of the markup.

The Committee moved to consideration of the managers' amendment by the Chairman, which was developed jointly by the Chairman and the Vice Chairman, and adopted the managers' amendment by a voice vote.

By a vote of 7 ayes to 8 noes, the Committee rejected an amendment by Senator Collins to require entities that own or control information systems that are deemed essential to the operation of designated critical infrastructure to report successful intrusions of those under certain circumstances. According to the amendment, such reporting would only be required with respect to systems where a cybersecurity incident could reasonably result in catastrophic regional or national effects on public health or safety, economic security, or national security. The votes in person or by proxy were as follows: Chairman Burr—no; Senator Risch—no; Senator Coats—aye; Senator Rubio—no; Senator Collins—aye; Senator Blunt—no; Senator Lankford—no; Senator Cotton—no; Vice Chairman Feinstein—no; Senator Wyden—no; Senator Mikulski—aye; Senator Warner— aye; Senator Heinrich—aye; Senator King—aye; Senator Hirono—aye.

By a vote of 3 ayes to 12 noes, the Committee rejected an amendment by Senator Wyden to prohibit the federal government from mandating that private companies deliberately introduce security weaknesses into their products. The votes in person or by proxy were as follows: Chairman Burr—no; Senator Coats—no; Senator Rubio—no; Senator Collins—no; Senator Blunt—no; Senator Lankford—no; Senator Cotton—no; Vice Chairman Feinstein—no;

Senator Wyden—aye; Senator Mikulski— no; Senator Warner— no; Senator Heinrich—aye; Senator King— no; Senator Hirono—aye.

By a voice vote, the Committee adopted an amendment by Senator Heinrich to require the Attorney General develop and make publicly available guidance to assist entities on the types of information that would qualify as cyber threat indicators under the bill and identify types of information that are protected under otherwise applicable privacy laws.

By a voice vote, the Committee adopted an amendment by Senator Hirono and Senator Rubio to place the Attorney General privacy guidelines on the same timeline as the bill requires for the Attorney General policies and procedures for the receipt of cyber threat indicators and defensive measures by the government. The amendment also requires the Attorney General to consult with private entities with industry expertise that are considered relevant before the promulgation of the final privacy guidelines.

Vote to report the committee bill

The Committee voted to report the bill as amended, by a vote of 14 ayes to 1 no. Chairman Burr—aye; Senator Risch—aye; Senator Coats—aye; Senator Rubio—aye; Senator Collins—aye; Senator Blunt—aye; Senator Lankford—aye; Senator Cotton—aye; Vice Chairman Feinstein—aye; Senator Wyden—no; Senator Mikulski—aye; Senator Warner—aye; Senator Heinrich—aye; Senator King—aye; Senator Hirono—aye.

COMPLIANCE WITH RULE XLIV

Rule XLIV of the Standing Rules of the Senate requires publication of a list of any "congressionally directed spending item, limited tax benefit, and limited tariff benefit" that is included in the bill or the committee report accompanying the bill. Consistent with the determination of the Committee not to create any congressionally directed spending items or earmarks, none have been included in the bill or this report. The bill and report also contain no limited tax benefits or limited tariff benefits.

ESTIMATE OF COSTS

Pursuant to paragraph 11(a)(1) of rule XXVI of the Standing Rules of the Senate, the Committee estimates that implementing the bill would have a discretionary cost of about $20 million over the 2015–2019 period, assuming appropriation of the necessary amounts. Enacting S. 754 would not affect direct spending or revenues; therefore pay-as-you-go procedures do not apply. On March 17, 2015, the Committee transmitted this bill to the Congressional Budget Office and requested it to conduct an estimate of the costs incurred in carrying out S. 754.

EVALUATION OF REGULATORY IMPACT

In accordance with paragraph 11(b) of rule XXVI of the Standing Rules of the Senate, the Committee finds that no substantial regulatory impact will be incurred by implementing the provisions of this legislation.

ADDITIONAL VIEWS OF SEN. HEINRICH AND SEN. HIRONO

The rising incidences of cyber attacks on our private and public networks increasingly threaten our economic and national security. Although the enactment of the Cybersecurity Information Sharing Act, or CISA, would not necessarily prevent such attacks, there is a general consensus that facilitating cybersecurity information sharing between the private sector and federal government would promote a common understanding of the threats we face and allow the private sector to more effectively defend its networks.

We supported the Cybersecurity Information Sharing Act during its consideration in the Senate Intelligence Committee because we support the broad aims of this bill. In particular, we agree that individuals, companies, and government institutions can best protect themselves from cyber-attacks when they are aware of the presence and nature of cyber threats. But the only way to ensure the broadest dissemination of threat information is to develop a framework in which that information can be shared and disseminated with appropriate restraints, guidance, and oversight.

The bill as passed out of the Committee provides more restraints, guidance, and oversight than did the earlier draft version of the legislation, including a narrowing of the definition and authorized use of defensive measures, fewer exceptions for liability protections for information shared outside of the DHS portal, and more limits on how cyber threat information is used.

In addition, we are pleased that the Committee adopted amendments we offered during the bill's markup. Senator Heinrich's amendment requires the Attorney General to develop guidance to help private sector companies understand the types of information typically considered to be cyber threat indicators, and the types of personal information generally considered unrelated to such a threat. Senator Hirono's amendment—offered with Senator Rubio—requires the privacy guidelines called for in the bill to be developed and promulgated in a timely and thorough manner, alongside the policies and procedures to be developed for the cyber threat information sharing program.

But we continue to harbor concerns about some of the bill's provisions. Vice Chairman Feinstein noted that the goal of the bill is for companies and the government to voluntarily share information about cybersecurity threats—not about personal information. Our concern is that, however well intended, the bill's provisions do not adequately direct companies to remove personally identifiable information when sharing cyber threat indicators with the government. The bill also lacks a directive that the Department of Homeland Security scrub cyber threat indicators for unnecessary personally identifiable information before sharing that information with other areas of the federal government. Further, the bill confers broad liability protections on companies before requiring them to abide by privacy guidelines. We believe that the privacy guidelines required in the bill should be treated as a serious component of the new cyber threat sharing regime—not as an afterthought—and thus should be promulgated before the liability protections in this legislation take effect.

Finally, we are unconvinced that it is necessary to create an entirely new exemption to the Freedom of Information Act, or FOIA. Government transparency is critical in order for citizens to hold their elected officials and bureaucrats accountable; however, the bill's inclusion of a new FOIA exemption is overbroad and unnecessary as the types of information shared with the government through this bill would already be exempt from unnecessary public release under current FOIA exemptions. And to the extent FOIA exemptions need to be updated, those changes should only be made following open hearings in which all stakeholders have an opportunity to have their voices heard.

We are committed to addressing some of these issues through amendments on the Senate floor, and believe there should be an open amendment process as this bill moves forward. A number of our colleagues on the Committee offered important amendments during the markup that we hope will be offered again for full Senate consideration—in particular, a number of those offered by Senator Wyden, and one by Sen. Collins to require mandatory reporting of cybersecurity intrusions for the most critical infrastructure owners and operators.

As with other countries around the world, the United States is still just beginning to find ways to confront and mitigate the very real dangers our country faces from cyber threats. Thus far, we have seen no perfect answers. But this bill is not intended to confront every threat. We support it as a way for the government and private sector to begin to address the shared threat that cyber attacks represent, and we will look forward to a robust debate on the floor.

ADDITIONAL VIEWS OF SENATOR COLLINS

The Cybersecurity Information Sharing Act of 2015 eliminates some of the legal and economic disincentives impeding voluntary two-way information sharing between private industry and government and is a first step in improving our nation's dangerously inadequate defenses against cyber attacks. This bill is insufficient, however, to protect the critical infrastructure of the American people who rely upon this infrastructure for their safety, health, and economic well-being. Simply put, the current threat posed by cyber actors is too great and the vulnerability of existing information systems operating critical infrastructure too widespread to depend solely upon voluntary measures to protect the most essential of these systems upon which our country and citizens depend.

Without information about intrusions into our most critical infrastructure, our government's ability to defend the country against advanced persistent threats will suffer in a domain where speed is critical. This threat is not theoretical. Admiral Mike Rogers, the director of the National Security Agency, has publicly discussed the cyber threat posed against critical infrastructure. In addition to stating his belief that U.S. Cyber Command will be tasked to help defend critical infrastructure, he has said that ''We have . . . observed intrusions into industrial control systems . . . what concerns us is that . . . capability can be used by nation-states, groups or individuals to take down the capability of the control systems.''

A tiered system of information sharing is part of the solution to address this significant vulnerability. The first tier of reporting should be voluntarily, rely upon the procedures established in this legislation, and be utilized by 99 percent of businesses. The second tier of reporting should be mandatory, and it should apply only to a subset of critical infrastructure where a cybersecurity incident could reasonably be expected to result in *catastrophic* regional or national effects on public health or safety, economic security, or national security.

For this reason, I offered an amendment during the Committee's consideration of the bill to implement this tiered system by requiring the small number of the owners and operators of the country's most critical infrastructure at greatest risk to report to the federal government intrusions of information systems essential to the operation of critical infrastructure.

Had my amendment been adopted, 99.99 percent of businesses and 96 percent of critical infrastructure would still decide for themselves whether or not to share information with the government. The four percent of critical infrastructure at greatest risk of a devastating cyber attack would be mandated to report successful cyber intrusions so the government can develop and deploy countermeasures to protect its networks and the information systems of other critical infrastructure.

The Department of Homeland Security has already identified 63 critical infrastructure entities where damage caused by a single cyber incident could reasonably result in $50 billion in economic damage or $25 billion in damage that occurs in conjunction with 2,500 immediate deaths or the severe degradation of our national security or defense. Public reporting by Mandiant in 2013 and repeated testimony of the Intelligence Community leave no doubt that U.S. critical infrastructure already faces advanced persistent cyber threats posed by nation-states and other actors.

The critical infrastructure of the United States remains woefully unprepared to confront this clear and present threat. One former agency head told the 9/11 Commission during its 10th anniversary review that, ''We are at September 10th levels in terms of cyber preparedness.'' We cannot afford to wait for a ''cyber 9/11'' before taking legislative action to protect our critical infrastructure. By rejecting my amendment, the Committee is electing to take just such a risk.

SUSAN M. COLLINS.

ADDITIONAL VIEWS OF SENATOR RON WYDEN

Cyber-attacks and hacking against U.S. companies and networks are a serious and growing problem, with very real consequences for American companies and American consumers, and pose a significant challenge for national security. I share my colleagues' view that Congress should do what it can to help address this problem. The most effective way to protect cybersecurity is to ensure that network owners take responsibility for security and effectively implement good security practices. And it is important to ensure that government agencies do not deliberately weaken security standards.

It also makes sense to encourage private companies to share information about cybersecurity threats. However, this information-sharing must include strong protections for the privacy rights of law-abiding American citizens. Any information-sharing legislation that lacks adequate privacy protections is not simply a cybersecurity bill, but a surveillance bill by another name.

I opposed this bill because I believe its insufficient privacy protections will lead to large amounts of personal information being shared with the government even when that information is not needed for cybersecurity. This could include email content, financial records, and a wide variety of other personal information. While corporations will have a choice about whether or not to participate in this sharing, they could do so without the knowledge or consent of their customers, and will be granted immunity from liability if they do so. Additionally, this bill trumps federal privacy laws and permits government agencies to use the collected information for a wide variety of purposes, rather than only to protect cybersecurity. The bill also creates a problematic double standard, in that personal information about individual consumers can be used for a variety of non-cybersecurity purposes, including law enforcement actions against those consumers, but information about the companies supplying the information generally may not be used to regulate those companies. A corporation's privacy is not more important than an individual's privacy.

This excessively broad collection may not be the intent of this bill, but the language is clearly drafted broadly enough to permit it. Most notably, the bill defines a cybersecurity threat as anything that ''may result'' in harm to a network. This broad definition will incentivize the sharing of information even when it is *unlikely* to pertain to an actual cybersecurity threat. A more tailored definition, limited to actions that are *reasonably likely* to harm or interfere with a network, would ensure that information-sharing is more narrowly focused on actual threats.

A more tailored approach would also specify that companies should only provide the government with individuals' personal information if it is necessary to describe a cybersecurity threat. This would discourage companies from unnecessarily sharing large amounts of their customers' private information. This bill unfortunately takes the opposite approach, and only requires private companies to withhold information that is *known* at the time of sharing to be personal information unrelated to cybersecurity. This approach will disincentivize companies from carefully reviewing the information that they share and lead to a much greater amount of personal information being transferred unnecessarily to law enforcement and intelligence agencies.

I am also concerned that this legislation does not provide individuals with an adequate mechanism for redress in cases where the government violates the rules established by this act. Similar bills have included provisions permitting individuals harmed by such violations to recover damages from the government, and such a provision is needed in this bill as well.

I am disappointed that the committee did not adopt stronger privacy protections in this legislation, and I am also disappointed that my amendment to prohibit government agencies from requiring U.S. hardware and software companies to build weaknesses into their products was not adopted. I have introduced this amendment as stand-alone legislation and will continue to pursue this goal.

This bill is likely to significantly increase government collection of individuals' personal information, while unfortunately doing relatively little to secure American networks. I hope to work with colleagues to address this bill's shortcomings, and if these flaws are not fixed I will continue to oppose it.

Finally, I remain very concerned that a secret Justice Department opinion that is of clear relevance to this debate continues to be withheld from the public. This opinion, which interprets common commercial service agreements, is inconsistent with the public's understanding of the law, and I believe it will be difficult for Congress to have a fully informed debate on cybersecurity legislation if it does not understand how these agreements have been interpreted by the Executive Branch.

I have repeatedly asked the Department of Justice to withdraw this opinion, and to release it to the public so that anyone who is a party to one of these agreements can consider whether their agreement should be revised. The deputy head of the Justice Department's Office of Legal Counsel testified to the Intelligence Committee that she would not rely on this opinion today, but I remain concerned that other government officials may be tempted to rely on it in the future. I will continue to press the Justice Department to release this opinion, so that Congress and the public can debate this bill with a full understanding of the facts. And I look forward to working with my colleagues to revise this legislation to ensure that Americans' privacy rights and American cybersecurity are both adequately protected.

CHANGES IN EXISTING LAWS

In the opinion of the Committee, it is necessary to dispense with the requirements of paragraph 12 of rule XXVI of the Standing Rules of the Senate in order to expedite the business of the Senate.